PRIMARY SOURCES OF THE THIRTEEN COLONIES AND THE LOST COLONY ™

A Primary Source History of the Colony of
MASSACHUSETTS

JERI FREEDMAN

rosen central
Primary Source™

The Rosen Publishing Group, Inc., New York

Published in 2006 by The Rosen Publishing Group, Inc.
29 East 21st Street, New York, NY 10010

Library of Congress Cataloging-in-Publication Data

Freedman, Jeri.
A primary source history of the Colony of Massachusetts / by Jeri Freedman.—1st ed.
   p. cm.—(Primary sources of the thirteen colonies and the Lost Colony)
Includes bibliographical references and index.
ISBN 1-4042-0428-8 (lib. bdg.)
ISBN 1-4042-0671-X (pbk. bdg.)
1. Massachusetts—History—Colonial period, ca. 1600-1775—Juvenile literature.
2. Massachusetts—History—1775-1865—Juvenile literature. 3. Massachusetts—History—Colonial period, ca. 1600-1775—Sources—Juvenile literature. 4. Massachusetts—History—1775-1865—Sources—Juvenile literature.
I. Title. II. Series.
F67.F74 2006
974.4'02–dc22

            2004030281

Manufactured in the United States of America

On the front cover: *The First Thanksgiving at Plymouth* painted in 1914 by Jennie A. Brownscombe (1850-1936).

CONTENTS

INTRODUCTION

The earliest settlers who came to the shores of Massachusetts from England were following a dream. Some were seeking a place where they could rule their own lives as they saw fit. Others were looking for the opportunity to become financially independent, mainly by owning land. All were looking for the opportunity to improve their way of life away from the regimented and tightly controlled society of Britain.

To understand colonial history in Massachusetts is to understand the unique nature of the United States. The concept that all people are equal and entitled to enjoy life, liberty, and the pursuit of their own goals (so long as they do not harm others) is a concept that those of us who grow up in the United States tend to take for granted. It is hard for us to imagine how unusual this outlook was in a world that was ruled by monarchs and a nobility with absolute power over the common people.

The Noble Experiment

The United States has been referred to as a "noble experiment" for precisely this reason. Although today, many nations throughout the world are democracies, at the time when the colonies in North America gained their independence, democracy was a revolutionary concept, and the leaders who fought so hard for freedom were radicals. The colonial history of Massachusetts is the history of the common people's attempt to gain control over their own destiny. From this, one can gain a greater appreciation for why the freedoms we enjoy today are so important.

Embarkation of the Pilgrims was re-created by Massachusetts artist Edgar Parker in 1875 from the original by Robert Weir for the Pilgrim Society. The pilgrims are depicted aboard the *Speedwell* gathered around the pastor John Robinson for a farewell service before their departure from Leiden, the Netherlands. Weapons and armor in the foreground symbolize the dangers that will be encountered in the New World. When William Bradford first used the term "pilgrim" to refer to the Separatists, he was quoting Hebrews, 11:13 " . . . that they were strangers and pilgrims on the earth" to describe the departure from Leiden.

But in Massachusetts, as in the other colonies, freedom and equality were not easily achieved. Only males who were full members of the church—"saints" as they were called—enjoyed all the privileges of the community, especially the right to vote. Prominent religious dissenters, like Roger Williams and Anne Hutchinson, were driven from the community. The native people of Massachusetts were brutally driven from their land. True democracy did not come naturally or easily, which perhaps makes the experiment all the more noble.

CHAPTER 1

A Journey of Faith

The first colonists who settled in Massachusetts were religious dissenters from England, the Puritans and the Pilgrims. These dissenters disagreed with the way that religion was practiced in England. They sought a place where they could live according to their own religious beliefs.

The reasons that these two groups came to Massachusetts are rooted in sixteenth-century England. In 1536, King Henry VIII (1491–1547) of England wanted to divorce his wife, with whom he had been unable to conceive a son, and remarry. When the pope refused his request, the king severed ties with the Roman Catholic Church. The king had Parliament declare him the supreme head of the Church of England. This was the beginning in England of the Reformation, the movement to reform, or purify, the Catholic Church. The Reformation had begun in Europe in 1517 with the protests of Martin Luther (1483–1546). The English Reformation resulted in conflict between the Protestant reformers and the Catholics in England, which continued from the sixteenth through the eighteenth centuries.

The Puritans disapproved of both the Catholic Church and the new Church of England, which they felt retained too many Catholic practices. John Foxe (1516–1587) was a priest, a scholar who had taught at Oxford University, and a tireless agitator for the purification of the Church of England. He is often credited with starting the Puritan movement. In 1563, he published a work called *Acts and Monuments*, which promptly became

Starting in 1536, King Henry VIII began the dissolution of the monasteries. In this eighteenth-century painting, his men are depicted confiscating religious property. Monasteries had been independent of government and loyal to the Catholic religion. They had also been wealthy due to endowments and land bestowed on them by rich barons. Henry VIII, having created the Church of England with himself as head, and in need of money for his wars with France and Scotland, began to audit these monasteries. This eventually led to dissolution—or redistribution—of the seized property to English gentry in return for support.

known as *The Book of Martyrs*. In this book, he recounted the suffering of English Protestant martyrs. The book then became a tool to rally people to the cause of purifying the Church of England. Foxe's book inspired the Puritan movement. The Puritans wanted to purify the church of such remnants of Catholicism as ornate ceremonies, its elaborate hierarchy that included bishops, and any and all beliefs and practices not specified in the Bible.

However, Queen Elizabeth I (1533-1603), who ruled England from 1558 to 1603, felt that the Puritans were a disruptive element. The Puritans were spied upon by the queen's secret police, and their meetings were broken up by the militia. Some of their leaders were imprisoned in the Tower of London, which was used as a prison at the time. By 1629, some of the Puritans decided to set out for the New World. On one hand they saw an opportunity to escape persecution in England. On the other hand, they saw the chance to create a community that would live in complete accordance with the Bible and provide salvation to the community's members.

A Separate Church

In contrast to the Puritans, the Pilgrims, also called the Separatists or Independents, were a "separatist group." They were alienated from both the Church of England and the Puritans. Robert Browne (1550-1633) is credited with starting this movement. A member of the Puritan movement, he became disillusioned with its unsuccessful attempts to change the Church of England. He decided that it was necessary to set up a separate, alternate church. In 1582, he wrote a book called *Reformation Without Tarrying for Anie* (Reformation Without Waiting for Anyone). This page explained the need for an immediate separation from the Church of England and the establishment of a new religious community. For instance, Browne and the Pilgrims held that there were only two true sacraments (means of receiving God's grace): baptism and the Lord's supper (communion). Because the Pilgrims refused to worship according to the Church of England, they were persecuted in the same way as the Puritans. In 1608, some of these Separatists, from a congregation in the village of Scrooby, England, decided to move to the Netherlands, which had a more tolerant religious atmosphere.

This is a title page of a pamphlet from the Virginia Company authored by a member of a party of adventurers who had returned from Virginia. The company sought investors. Page 11 of the discourse reads, "The ayre and clymate most sweete and wholsome, much warmer then *England*, and very agreeable to our Natures: It is inhabited with wild and savage people . . . they have no law but nature, their apparell skinnes of beasts, but most goe naked . . . they are generally very loving and gentle, and doe entertaine and relieve our people with great kindnesse: they are easy to be brought to good . . ."

The Promise of Earthly Rewards

Although they could practice their religion freely, life in the Netherlands wasn't easy for the Pilgrims. Many of them lacked training in skilled trades. They were forced to earn their living through poorly paid, hard manual labor. At the same time, as their children grew older, many of them started to absorb Dutch culture rather than follow the religious ways of their parents. On top of all this, by 1620, military hostilities were threatening to flare up between the Netherlands and Spain. The Pilgrims felt that the time had come to seek a new sanctuary.

By the early seventeenth century, English merchants began to join together in investment companies to send colonists to the New World. The colonists would provide the merchants with the marketable commodities found there, such as wood and furs. A standard agreement was that in return for the cost of their passage and supplies, the colonists would labor for free for seven years and would send commodities back to England, where they could be sold at a profit. At the end of the seven years, the colonist would receive a grant of land of his own.

One such company was the Virginia Company of London. In 1607, the Virginia Company founded the first successful British colony in the New World, at Jamestown in Virginia. In order to attract colonists, the companies and the British crown had to promote life in the colonies. They advertised the New World as a land of wondrous beauty; plentiful, unpopulated land; and abundant resources. For those with no property and little opportunity, like the members of the lower and middle classes in England, the New World sounded like a paradise.

A Voyage of Faith

The Pilgrims were among those attracted by these accounts of life in Virginia. In August 1620, it carried them from the Netherlands back to England, where they joined co-religionists upon the *Mayflower*, bound for Virginia. The *Mayflower* departed Plymouth, England, on September 6, 1620, carrying 102 passengers including soldiers, servants, and adventurers, as well as the Pilgrims. It took the *Mayflower* about sixty-six days to cross 2,750 miles (4,426 kilometers) of the Atlantic Ocean.

The passengers on the *Mayflower* did not plan to land in Massachusetts. Blown off-course by stormy weather, they landed

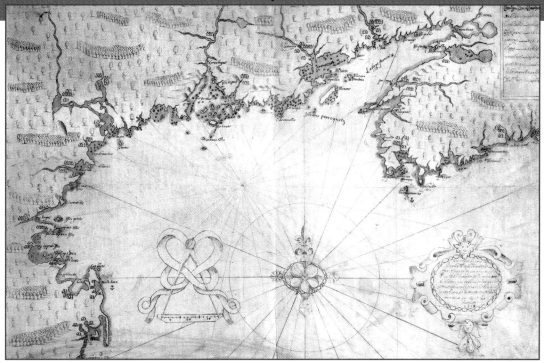

The French explorer and navigator Samuel de Champlain (1567–1635) is considered the founder of New France. This map, created in 1607, provides the first delineation of the New England coast and the Canadian coast from western Nova Scotia to Cape Cod. This map is also unique in that Champlain drew it himself, not relying on the services of a professional cartographer in Europe to illustrate from notes of his observations. He created this map on vellum based on his own explorations and interviews he conducted with Native Americans.

much farther north than they intended, well outside the boundaries of Virginia.

The Pilgrims found themselves off the coast of Cape Cod on November 19, 1620. The weather was getting worse, and attempting to continue farther south down the coast toward their original destination was too dangerous. So they dropped anchor at what is now Provincetown, Massachusetts.

Because they were not in Virginia, the terms of the Pilgrims' agreement with the Virginia Company no longer applied.

Governor William Bradford created the list of passengers aboard the *Mayflower* for his *Of Plymouth Plantation*. This is the first page of the passenger list from a facsimile of the original document. Edward Winslow, whose name appears on a later page of the list, posed for this portrait *(inset)* in London on one of his last visits to the city in 1651. It is the only surviving portrait to exist of a *Mayflower* passenger. Winslow would serve as the third governor of the colony of Plymouth. He died at sea on a voyage from Hispaniola to Jamaica on May 8, 1655.

Accordingly, forty-one men aboard the *Mayflower* drew up a new agreement, the Mayflower Compact. The compact proclaimed the colonists' continued loyalty to the British crown. It committed its signers to joining together to create a government and laws for the new colony. Because of this shared commitment to self-rule, many historians regard the Mayflower Compact to be the first written constitution in the Americas.

CHAPTER 2

Life in a New Land

For five weeks, most of the colonists remained on the *Mayflower* while Captain Miles Standish (1584–1656) led a small group of men to explore the area where they had landed. The party finally located a suitable spot for landing and setting up a colony opposite the tip of Cape Cod. The area contained suitable land for farming and a stream for fresh water. Over several days beginning on December 20, 1620, groups of Pilgrims went ashore into the Massachusetts winter. The Native American name of the place they landed was Patuxet. The Pilgrims called it New Plymouth (later shortened to just Plymouth) after the town of Plymouth in England.

On the site of an abandoned Native American village, the Pilgrims began constructing the first buildings of their settlement. They had to build quickly, for the harsh New England winter had already begun. Only fifty-two of the original 102 colonists would survive until spring. The rest succumbed to exposure, fatigue, illness, injury, and hunger. The future of the colony seemed doubtful.

Help from an Unexpected Source

In the spring of 1621, assistance arrived in a surprising way. The local Wampanoag Indians, whose name means "people of the dawn," offered to help the English colonists.

In the fall and winter, the Wampanoags lived in the forest. There they hunted deer, wild turkeys, otters, and a variety of other animals. In the spring they moved to the shore. They then fished and planted crops, such as corn, beans, and squash, on the open land. Now they had returned to their spring settlement.

This is how late-nineteenth-century artist W. L. Williams imagined the colony of Plymouth looked in 1622. No original Pilgrim house survives (the earliest still standing dates from 1640). The houses here are depicted to be rather large among a very landscaped scene. However, the depiction of the settlement's size may be accurate. Archaeological excavations have uncovered evidence of wooden homes with corner posts fixed into the ground. The roofs of the homes were made of thatch, which shed water well. The homes had earthen floors, one or two rooms with a loft space for children and servants to sleep, and only a few small windows.

The Wampanoag population had already declined significantly by the time the Pilgrims arrived. Like many of the other tribes in the region, the Wampanoags had lost many people to diseases brought to the New World by European explorers. In addition, the tribe had been carrying on a war with the neighboring Narragansett Indians. This war had resulted in the loss of many Wampanoags.

Tribal chief Massasoit saw the English colonists as potential allies who might help his people in their war with the Narragansett and Massachusett nations. He entered into a treaty with the Pilgrims. By and large, the two groups maintained peaceful relations for a number of years.

The Wampanoags provided valuable advice to the Pilgrims that helped them survive in their new home. One of the most important things the Wampanoags taught the Pilgrims was how to grow native crops such as corn, beans, and squash, which provided critically needed food. Because of the treaty, the Pilgrims could harvest these crops safely. In appreciation, they killed some wild turkeys and held the first Thanksgiving. Relations with the Native Americans would soon grow more troubled, however.

Life in the Colony

William Bradford was most well known as the governor of the Plymouth Colony, a post he held for more than thirty years. His *Of Plymouth Plantation* provides a valuable source of information about life in the colony. The Plymouth Colony developed a healthy trade with England in furs and fish. As the soil in Massachusetts was rocky and the weather cooler than in the southern colonies, the colony never experienced the same type of financial success as southern colonies such as Virginia. Nonetheless, it survived, and the religious faithful were able to live their lives according to their principles.

The Massachusetts Bay Colony

For those religious dissenters who remained in England, the 1620s was a period of great strife. In 1625, Charles I succeeded King James I as ruler of England. Determined that the monarch,

The Pilgrims had only seen the Native Americans from a distance, until approached by Samoset on March 1, 1621, followed by Massasoit. Above is a depiction of the encounter with Massasoit entitled *Interview with Massasoit* by nineteenth-century illustrator Seth Eastman. Massasoit was one of the most powerful leaders, or sachems, in New England. The Wampanoag nation, of which Massasoit's tribe of Pokanoket belonged, extended from present-day Boston to Narragansett Bay, Rhode Island. The inset picture shows a re-creation of a *wetu*, or Wampanoag home. The *wetu* was made of straw mats stretched over a wooden frame, and the Wampanoags carried the straw layers with them when they relocated seasonally.

rather than Parliament, should be the primary authority in England, Charles disbanded Parliament in 1630. He introduced new persecutions of religious dissenters.

Frustrated by the new persecution, in 1628 a group of Puritan businessmen decided that America offered a better opportunity. They formed the Massachusetts Bay Company and received a land grant from the necessary authorities. A colony was established in Massachusetts Bay on the Shawmut Peninsula, near the later site of the city of Boston.

The Puritan Migration

The largest emigration of Puritans from England to Massachusetts, called the Great Migration, began in 1630. Over the next decade, about 14,000 Puritans immigrated to Massachusetts. All told, 20,000 English immigrated to Massachusetts in the seventeenth century. This was a small number compared to the 120,000 English who immigrated to the Chesapeake colonies (Virginia and Maryland) during that time and the 190,000 who immigrated to the West Indies. English immigration to Massachusetts essentially stopped after the Great Migration. The colony's population increased after that period by natural growth rather than through continued immigration.

Most, but not all, of these new Massachusetts colonists were Puritans. About 60 percent of them came from nine counties in east England. These Massachusetts colonists differed from other colonists in many ways. They tended to be middle class rather than poor. They worked in a trade (such as carpentry, weaving, or mining) rather than in agriculture. The Puritans were able to read and write. Also, they paid their own way rather than came as indentured servants. A larger percentage of these Massachusetts colonists were women.

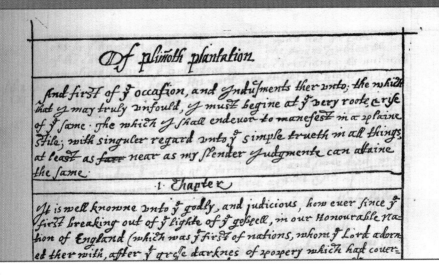

William Bradford's journal would become the most complete surviving source on life for the Pilgrims between 1630 and 1647. It begins with year 1608, at the time they settled in the Netherlands, and ends with the second *Mayflower* passenger list that includes the fate of each passenger. Historians of the seventeenth and eighteenth centuries had access to the original manuscript, located for a time at the Old South Church in Boston. It disappeared and was rediscovered in London in the 1850s. The journal was finally returned to Massachusetts in 1897. See pages 54–55 for a transcription of this introduction and an additional excerpt.

Once in Massachusetts, the Puritans tended to settle in compact towns, where they could establish churches and local government. Some of these towns were Newtown (Cambridge), Lexington, Concord, Charlestown, Dorchester, and Watertown.

The Covenant with God

The Puritans believed that only a select few, known as the elect, had been chosen by God to escape eternal damnation. They believed that it was their responsibility to God and to others to see that God's laws were enforced. The good of the entire community depended on this ability to regulate individual behavior. Living together, in small towns and close-knit family groups, allowed for such tight regulation. Those who dissented from

These are copperplate engravings by Wenceslaus Hollar from *Ornatus Muliebris Anglicanus*, or the Severall Habits of English Women, published in 1648 in London. They depict the style of dress of an English Puritan woman. This is most likely the style of dress of the newly immigrated Puritans in the New World. There, laws were passed forbidding people to dress in a showy fashion or in a manner inappropriate for their social station.

Puritan teachings, such as Roger Williams and Anne Hutchinson, were driven out of the colony.

The Puritans felt it was important for people to be able to read so that they could read the Bible. Parents were required to see that their children were taught to read. Therefore, along with a church, virtually every Massachusetts town maintained its own public school. Seventeenth-century Massachusetts also featured the highest rate of book ownership in the world. Most of these were Bibles and other religious publications. Not surprisingly, the first printing press in the English colonies was established in

Massachusetts, in the town of Cambridge, in 1640. Four years earlier, also at Cambridge, the Puritans had founded the first college in the colonies—Harvard—for the purpose of training preachers.

The Pequot War and King Philip's War

Native Americans were not part of the Puritans' covenant with God. The Puritans saw the heavily wooded New England countryside as a "howling wilderness" more than an unspoiled paradise. The Native Americans had their own way of living on and using the land. Yet the Puritans saw the Indians' failure to clear and plant fields, build permanent residences and towns, or establish a concept of individual ownership of property as evidence that they were savage heathens who had no rights to the land's benefits.

As the colony's English population grew, conflict with the Native Americans increased. Although outnumbered at first, the colonists possessed the advantage of superior weaponry, in the form of guns. They were able to use longtime quarrels between the different tribes, such as the Pequots, Wampanoags, and Narragansetts, to their own advantage. In 1637, a colonist force ambushed a sleeping Pequot village along the Mystic River and set it afire just before dawn. Only five of the Pequots survived the inferno. William Bradford, governor of the Plymouth colony, wrote that though "it was a fearful sight to see [the Pequots] thus frying in the fire and the streams of blood . . . horrible was the stink and scent," victory nonetheless seemed "a sweet sacrifice."

The Pequot War terrorized the Native American population of Massachusetts. King Philip's War, fought by the colonists against the Wampanoags and Narragansetts in 1675 to 1676, was even more devastating. It ended with the head of the Wampanoag chief

In 1692, three young girls familiar with Puritan leader Reverend Cotton Mather's book *Memorable Providences Relating to Witchcrafts and Possessions* accused a West Indian slave named Tituba of practicing witchcraft in Salem. After being beaten, Tituba confessed to being a witch. This led to a craze that did not stop until the community's rich and powerful began to be accused. Above is a petition from ten women and a few men who were being held without trial, requesting to be released on bail. Tompkins Harrison Matteson's 1853 painting *Examination of a Witch* depicts a midwife pointing at a "witch's mark" on an accused woman's back. See page 55 for a transcription.

Metacom (known to the colonists as King Philip) displayed publicly on a watchtower at Plymouth. One-third of the Native Americans was killed. Many more were sold into slavery in the West Indies. Others fled into the northern wilderness. The remainder were herded into "praying villages" where they were converted to Christianity. All in all, one in ten soldiers on both sides was injured or killed. King Philip's War was one of the bloodiest and most costly in America's history.

CHAPTER 3

Enlightenment and Oppression

By the 1690s, a new era was dawning in Massachusetts. The population had grown to between 50,000 and 60,000. Massachusetts was a colony of self-sufficient farms, but thrived from trade, particularly with the English colonies in the West Indies. Shipbuilding was an extremely important part of the economy. By 1700, Boston shipyards built more ships than all the other English colonies combined. They built more than anywhere else in the British empire except for London. Commercial fishing, particularly for cod, and the "carrying trade"—transporting cargo by ship—was also important.

Colony or Competitor?

Massachusetts's growing wealth did not always please England. The mother country still tended to regard the Massachusetts colonists as dangerous dissenters and heretics and resented the colonists' belief that they represented a "purified" form of English society. Unlike Virginia and the West Indies, Massachusetts did not devote its economy to producing a commodity, such as tobacco or sugar, that was in great demand in England. Instead, Massachusetts's trade with the Indies made it a direct competitor of England for those markets and commodities. English resentment grew as the Crown, in the 1760s, became increasingly desperate for revenues to fund its global wars with France for colonies.

Edmund Burke (*left*) was an English statesman who came to the colonies' defense in Parliament. He argued that Britain's traditional ruling practice was necessary for an orderly, stable society. Moreover, he saw Britain's inflexibility in regard to the colonies as leading to unrest and revolution. By cooperating with the colonies and being willing to change, he argued that it would reaffirm tradition and values. Lord North (*right*) continued to take a hard stand against the American colonies. He resigned as prime minister in 1782 due to the loss of America.

King George III

King George III (1738–1820) assumed the throne in 1760. King George felt that his predecessors had allowed too much power to be shifted from the monarchy to the people. He wished to restore more power to the monarchy. In 1770, he appointed Lord Frederick North (1713–1792) as prime minister. Lord North shared the king's views. They put forth a series of policies that slowly and certainly drove America toward revolution and war.

25

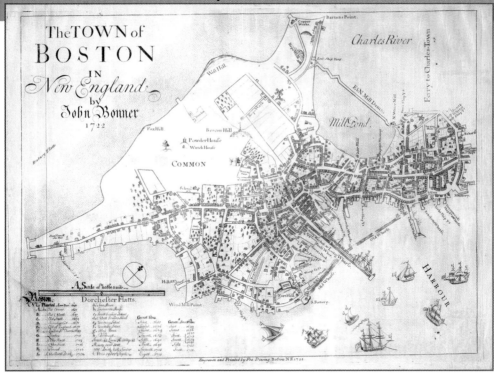

This is the first town plan to be printed in the colonies. It is also the first surviving map of Boston. Printed in 1722, it depicts nearly 100 years of development since the city was founded in 1630. At the time, Boston had a population of 12,000 and was the largest city in British North America. The map was created by Captain John Bonner. The chart at the bottom of the map lists the dates of smallpox epidemics, great fires, and when many buildings were constructed.

Cash for the Crown

England's wars with France left England with a huge debt. Since their founding, the colonies had always claimed the right to tax themselves through their own elected colonial assemblies. Now the British government decided to increase its revenues by directly taxing the colonies.

Among the first tax acts imposed on the colonies was the Revenue Act of 1764, also called the Sugar Act. This imposed a tax on sugar, as well as a variety of other items including cloth, coffee, tropical foods, fabrics such as silk, and wine.

The enforcement of this tax caused great hardship in the colonies. A major colonial export of the day was rum, which was distilled from imported sugar products. As the cost of importing sugar increased, the production of rum decreased along with colonial income. Angry New England rum distillers agitated for a boycott of imported English goods.

Since the American colonists had no representatives in the British parliament, they needed another strong source of support if they were to get any attention. The colonists believed that if they could cause a decline in trade among English merchants, these influential men would force the government to change its taxation policy in the colonies. The proposal for a ban on the importation of English goods, called a nonimportation agreement, was approved at a Boston town meeting. The boycott subsequently spread throughout New England and New York. Taxed already by their own assemblies, the colonies resented being taxed by Parliament, in which they had no direct representatives.

The Stamp Act

In 1765, the British parliament further angered the colonists by enacting the Stamp Act. This law imposed a tax in the form of a stamp required on virtually all published material and legal and official documents. Opposition to the stamp tax in the colonies was immediate and violent.

Chaos at Home and Abroad

Demonstrations took place throughout the colonies. Merchants refused to sell British goods. Massachusetts colonists who

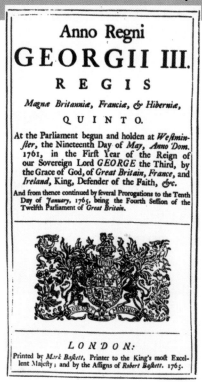

The title page of the first edition of the Stamp Act in January 1765 is pictured here. The Stamp Act was the first direct tax imposed on the colonies. Newspapers, legal documents, ship papers, and even playing cards were to be embossed with the stamp (*right*) that was manufactured for the act. The amount of this tax was relatively small. However, it was troubling to the colonists that it was passed in Parliament without debate, without the colonies having a representative in Parliament, and could open the door for more taxes against the colonies in the future. Massachusetts took the lead in organizing resistance to the law.

opposed the Stamp Act came to be known as the Sons of Liberty, a term that had been used before for various British groups organized to protest government policies.

Samuel Adams (1722–1803) was a leader in the Massachusetts Sons of Liberty. Adams, born in Quincy, Massachusetts, was the son of a prosperous brewer and landowner. He graduated from Harvard College and started to study law, but gave it up to go to work for one of the colony's most prominent merchants. He soon

This portrait of Samuel Adams was painted circa 1770 to 1772. Adams's father had been a wealthy brewer until an investment he made in a paper currency venture failed, due to the British government declaring such an act illegal in 1744. This event may have sparked a dislike for central government in the family, leading Adams to become a revolutionary and organizer against Britain. After he retired from Congress in 1781, he returned to Massachusetts where he eventually was elected governor and served for many years, until he retired for health reasons.

quit, however, and devoted himself to politics. In 1765, he was elected to represent Boston in the General Court, which was the Massachusetts legislature. A tireless organizer of efforts to resist the pressures from the English, he became a major leader in the cause for independence from England.

Led by men such as Adams and James Otis (1725–1783), the Sons of Liberty made sure that people observed boycotts of English goods. Sometimes they resorted to violence such as bullying those charged with unloading and distributing taxed goods. They also led public protests against English policies. They organized protests in

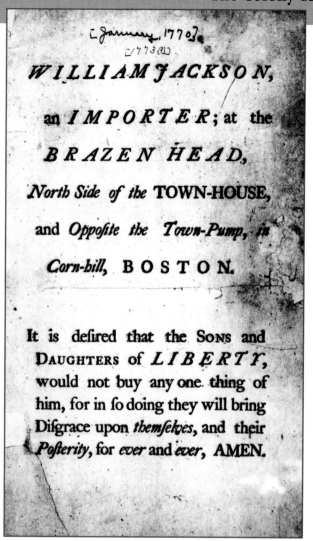

January, 1770.
(/773(1)

WILLIAM JACKSON,

an IMPORTER; at the

BRAZEN HEAD,

North Side of the TOWN-HOUSE,

and Opposite the Town-Pump, in

Corn-hill, BOSTON.

It is desired that the SONS and
DAUGHTERS of LIBERTY,
would not buy any one thing of
him, for in so doing they will bring
Disgrace upon themselves, and their
Posterity, for ever and ever, AMEN.

This broadside distributed to the Boston-area "sons and daughters of liberty" called for a boycott on the goods sold by Willam Jackson, a Boston tradesman who had not complied with the boycott on British imported goods. The first Sons of Liberty was formed in New York City and was mostly made up of upper middle–class colonists. After a similar group formed in Massachusetts, groups formed in Virginia, Georgia, and the Carolinas. After temporarily waning in most of the colonies after the Stamp Act was repealed, the movement was revived to fight the Townshend Acts.

Boston against the Stamp Act, and these demonstrations frightened England's representative responsible for distributing the stamps so much that he resigned. The Sons of Liberty's strong-arm techniques made it impossible to enforce the Stamp Act. In November 1766, the British government repealed the Stamp Act, largely because of pressure from English merchants who were suffering from the colonial boycott on British products.

CHAPTER 4

After the Stamp Act was repealed, Britain decided instead to impose taxes on items such as lead, paper, paint, glass, and tea. In response, the Massachusetts colonists once again implemented a nonimportation boycott of English goods. This boycott was initiated by a circular letter written in February 1768 by Samuel Adams on behalf of the Massachusetts House of Representatives, part of the General Court, which was the representative assembly of Massachusetts.

Rebellion in the Air

In 1772, Samuel Adams set up the Boston Committee of Correspondence to keep people in the colony informed about political events and activities. Many other colonial assemblies subsequently created Committees of Correspondence. These committees spread the word about actions of local assemblies and sent out calls for political action.

The Boston Massacre

In response to the constant unrest, the British sent 4,000 soldiers to Boston. The Bostonians bristled at the arrival of the soldiers, and clashes between the residents and the soldiers were common. In March 1770, several local youths got into an altercation with a soldier on guard at the customs house. The sentry struck one of the youths with his musket. An angry crowd gathered and began pelting the British soldiers with snowballs and other objects. In response, the British soldiers opened fire, killing five colonists and wounding several more. Among those killed was Crispus Attucks, the first black man to die in the escalating conflict between the colonists and the British. Radical Bostonians

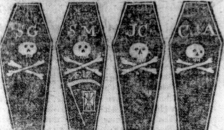

There is much debate among historians as to the ancestry of Crispus Attucks. Some speculate that he was a mix of Natick Indian and African. He is also believed to have been a runaway slave. Attucks's initials can be found on the coffin *(far right)* in this obituary that appeared in the *Boston Gazette* on March 12, 1770. He had been eating dinner when he heard fighting between Boston men and the British soldiers. Upon arriving at the scene, Attucks struck at one of the soldiers, who then fired two muskets at him, killing him. See pages 55–56 for transcription of the full obituary.

such as Samuel Adams used the so-called Boston Massacre to gather support for the cause of revolution among other colonists.

The Boston Tea Party

Following the Boston Massacre, Parliament repealed most of the taxes on the colonies except for one on tea. In response, the Massachusetts colonists refused to buy tea brought to the colony on British ships, relying instead on tea they smuggled in from the Far East on their own ships. The colonial boycott on tea caused tea sales in the colonies to drop by 70 percent, badly damaging the finances of British tea companies. In an effort to keep the British East India Tea Company from going bankrupt, the Tea Act was passed by Parliament in 1773. This act gave the company a monopoly on the sale of tea to the colonies and allowed it to sell the tea at a very low price. The British figured that colonists wouldn't object to paying the tea tax if they could get it very cheaply.

The radical colonists, led by Samuel Adams, were determined to block the British plan. The first tea-bearing ship operating under the act, the *Dartmouth*, arrived in Boston on November 28. Adams led meetings at the Old South Meeting House in Boston, inciting the colonists against the idea of British taxation. Late one night a group of men, disguised as Native Americans to make it hard to identify them, boarded the *Dartmouth*, the *Beaver*, and the *Eleanor*. They broke open the chests and dumped the tea into the harbor. The Boston Tea Party infuriated the king and Parliament.

Coercion

Britain had lost patience with its rebellious colonists, particularly those in Massachusetts. Its response was what were popularly called the Coercive Acts in Britain and the Intolerable Acts in America passed in 1774. These included the following:

- **Massachusetts Government Act**: This act restricted town meetings in Massachusetts and replaced elected officials with royal appointees.

- **Administration of Justice Act**: This act gave British officials accused of crimes in the colonies the right to be tried in Britain (effectively allowing them to escape punishment in many cases).

A total of forty-five tons of tea was dumped into Boston Harbor on December 16, 1773. The band of Patriots was quiet and orderly in the execution of its plot as were the thousands of spectators at Griffin's wharf. The only sound reportedly heard was of the axes and hatchets striking the wood of more than 340 wooden crates. Some citizens attempted to grab handfuls of the tea leaves and hide them in their pockets. The next morning, large quantities were floating on the water. Sailors in small boats pushed them down into the water with their oars. One surviving artifact is this glass bottle *(inset)* filled with leaves.

- **Quartering Act**: This act required people to house British soldiers in their homes.

- **Boston Port Act**: This act closed the port of Boston until the city paid for the tea destroyed and the damage to the customs offices. Boston also had to acknowledge that Parliament had the right to assess taxes on commodities such as tea. It effectively cut off all trade to and from Boston, causing much hardship in the colony.

In response to the Coercive Acts, Samuel Adams and the Boston Committee of Correspondence circulated a letter to the other colonies. This letter claimed Massachusetts was being cruelly and unfairly oppressed by the British.

Many people in other colonies agreed with Samuel Adams. The Coercive Acts enormously increased sympathy and respect for the colony of Massachusetts among other colonists. The harshness of the acts convinced many politically moderate people in Massachusetts who had been reluctant to support the Massachusetts rebels that perhaps the radicals were justified.

The Suffolk Resolves

In September 1774, a group of men from Boston and other towns in Suffolk County drafted the Suffolk Resolves, a series of resolutions that expressed the feelings of the rebels as follows: "That it is an indispensable duty which we owe to God, our country, ourselves and posterity, by all lawful ways and means in our power to maintain, defend and preserve those civil and religious rights and liberties, for which many of our fathers fought, bled and died, and to hand them down entire to future generations." Among other things, the resolves stated that the Coercive Acts were unconstitutional. Taxes collected in Massachusetts should be kept by the local Massachusetts government rather than sent to Britain. These resolves also stated that the people of Massachusetts should create a local militia, arm it, and begin weekly drills.

The First Continental Congress

In response to the Coercive Acts, the First Continental Congress was held in Philadelphia from September 5 to October 26, 1774. Representatives from Massachusetts included Samuel Adams and his cousin John Adams (1735–1826), who would later become the second president of the United States. A copy of the Suffolk Resolves was presented to the members of the congress. At first some attendees thought the resolves were too radical and would lead to war. However, in the end they were passed. The congress enacted the Declaration and Resolves of the First Continental Congress, addressed to King George III, which stated the following:

- The colonists were "entitled to life, liberty and property: and they have never ceded to any foreign power whatever, a right to dispose of either without their consent."

- The colonists' ancestors, "who first settled these colonies, were at the time of their emigration from the mother country, entitled to all the rights, liberties, and immunities of free and natural-born subjects, within the realm of England."

- Since the colonists did not have representation in the British legislature, they were entitled to have their own, and they should only be taxed by that provincial legislature.

- "The keeping [of] a standing army in these colonies, in times of peace, without the consent of the legislature of that colony, in which such army is kept, is against law."

- The repressive acts imposed by Parliament were an attempt to enslave the colonies.

The First Continental Congress enacted a total ban on importation of products from anywhere in the British Empire. The ban had a provision that if Parliament did not revoke the Coercive Acts by December 1, 1774, the colonies would also stop exporting goods to Britain.

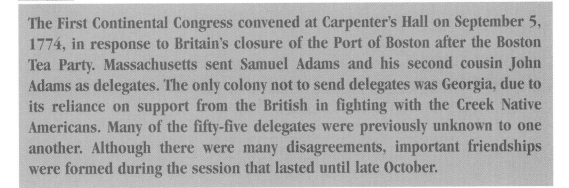

The First Continental Congress convened at Carpenter's Hall on September 5, 1774, in response to Britain's closure of the Port of Boston after the Boston Tea Party. Massachusetts sent Samuel Adams and his second cousin John Adams as delegates. The only colony not to send delegates was Georgia, due to its reliance on support from the British in fighting with the Creek Native Americans. Many of the fifty-five delegates were previously unknown to one another. Although there were many disagreements, important friendships were formed during the session that lasted until late October.

Parliament responded with the New England Restraining Act. This stated that the trade of the New England colonies would be limited to importing and exporting goods to and from England and the British West Indies. Eventually the terms of the act were extended to cover other colonies that joined with New England in boycotting English goods.

CHAPTER 5

The call for a colonial militia had been heeded throughout Massachusetts. Citizens had begun stockpiling weapons to use in case the conflict with England flared into open warfare. The members of the colonial militia were called minutemen because they were ordinary citizens who had vowed that, if necessary, they would drop whatever they were doing and be ready to fight at a minute's notice.

War!

The spark that would ignite the Revolutionary War was struck on April 19, 1775, in the villages of Lexington and Concord, located a few miles west of Boston. Many of the colonial leaders had been hiding in the area, seeking to avoid capture by the British. They had not lost touch with events in Boston, however.

Paul Revere's Ride

Paul Revere (1735–1818) was a Boston silversmith and engraver of printing plates used to print pictures. He was a member of the Boston Committee of Correspondence and carried news and correspondence from Massachusetts to the other colonies. While some rebel leaders hid in the outlying towns around Boston, Revere remained in the city going about his usual business activities and acting as a messenger between Boston and the outlying communities where the rebel leaders were hiding.

In April 1775, the rebels observed an increase in activity among the British army in Boston. This led them to believe that the British were preparing to move against the rebels in communities west of Boston. Revere met secretly with the rebel leaders and came up with a plan to alert them of the route by which the British would advance.

This iconic painting by famous colonial artist John Singleton Copley (1738–1815) portrays Paul Revere as the craftsman, although by this time he was also well established in the world of politics and had gained his reputation as an impassioned Patriot. Here, Revere is holding a teapot and seems to be contemplating what to engrave on it. Teapots were the most expensive items made by Revere. The teapot is symbolic because Copley painted this at the time of the Townshend Acts, which imposed heavy taxes on tea.

Revere and the rebel leaders were aware that it might be impossible for Revere to get out of Boston during a British advance. They came up with a plan relying on lanterns placed in the belfry of the Old North Church, whose light could be seen across the Charles River by the rebels. One lantern would indicate that the British were approaching by land across Boston Neck, then marching northwest toward Concord. Two lanterns would indicate that the British were crossing the Charles River by boat from Boston to Cambridge, then moving west to Concord.

On the evening of April 18, 1775, colonial spies observed that the British soldiers were getting boats ready to leave Boston via the Charles River. Around 10 PM, Revere and a local shoemaker, William Dawes (1745–1799), took off to warn the rebels. Dawes set off by land crossing Roxbury, Brookline, and

Cambridge. To increase the possibility that one of them would succeed in reaching Lexington, Revere took a different route. He crossed the Charles River into Charlestown, then rode west by horse, narrowly escaping capture by the British at Charlestown Neck.

Revere and Dawes both arrived in Lexington. They woke up Samuel Adams and John Hancock (1737–1793), who were sleeping at the house of Jonas Clark. John Hancock was one of the richest men in the colony, but when the Stamp Act was imposed, he had taken sides with those urging resistance rather than standing with his fellow businessmen. Revere reported to Hancock and Adams, "The Regulars are coming!" (referring to the British Regular Army soldiers).

By the morning, seventy-seven of the local minutemen had gathered at the Buckman Tavern near the Lexington Common. The British arrived around dawn. When the commander of the British forces saw how few soldiers the Americans had, he ordered them to disperse.

The leader of the minutemen, Captain John Parker, told them, "Stand your ground; don't fire unless fired upon, but if they mean to have a war, let it begin here."

Suddenly a shot was fired—no one is sure by whom. The response was instantaneous—both sides opened fire. Eight Americans were killed and ten wounded. One British soldier was wounded. Clearly outmanned, the American militiamen retreated into the woods. Shortly after midnight the British soldiers advanced from Lexington toward Concord to institute a search for weapons that the colonials had hidden there.

Meanwhile, Dawes and Revere, along with Dr. Samuel Prescott of Concord, set out to warn the minutemen at Concord. En route the three encountered a British roadblock. Dawes and Revere

This copper engraving is one of four plates created by Amos Doolittle and painted by his friend and cohort, Ralph Earl. Doolittle and Earl were among the ranks of the volunteer army that arrived in Cambridge, Massachusetts, upon hearing the news of the fighting that had erupted on April 19, 1775. They received permission to investigate the sites of the recent fighting. There, they interviewed witnesses and participants and made sketches. The second plate in the series, above, is titled *A View of the Town of Concord*.

were captured, but Prescott used his familiarity with the local countryside to evade the British and arrived at Concord to alert the militia. Church bells were sounded, which signaled to the minutemen that they should assemble. They poured in from the surrounding towns of Bedford, Littleton, Westford, Carlisle, Chelmsford, and Acton.

The minutemen met the British forces at the Old North Bridge, which crosses over the Concord River. Shots were fired, and two Americans were killed. The American force was larger than in Lexington and had no intention of backing down. The

41

From their hilltop vantage point, the militia force of more than 400 men saw smoke billowing from Concord and assumed their homes had been torched. The British had only made a bonfire of the artillery. Upon return to town, it was at this site at the Old North Bridge that the minutemen confronted the British. The British attempted to remove loose pilings of the bridge to impede the minutemen's march back into Concord. The original structure of the bridge has long since been dismantled and reconstructed.

minutemen returned fire, and the British were forced to retreat toward Lexington.

The Second Continental Congress

Following the battles at Lexington and Concord, the Second Continental Congress convened in May 1775. Even as minutemen continued to pour into the areas near Boston, the congress began its work. John Hancock was elected president of the congress. The rest of the Massachusetts delegation consisted of John

Adams, Thomas Cushing (1725-1788; later replaced by Elbridge Gerry (1744-1814)), and Robert Treat Paine (1731-1814).

The congress formally took control of the army amassing near Boston. George Washington was appointed head of the Continental army and was sent to Boston. Richard Henry Lee (1732-1794) of Virginia introduced a resolution stating that the colonies should be free and separate from England. John Adams argued forcefully for its approval. The resolution passed, and Thomas Jefferson was appointed to create the Declaration of Independence. It was signed by the members of the Massachusetts delegation on July 4, 1776, and a copy was sent to Boston. When it arrived, the Massachusetts House of Representatives had it read from the balcony of the State House on State Street in downtown Boston.

The Defense of Boston

Following the battle at Concord, the commander of the British troops, Thomas Gage, withdrew his troops to Boston. The Continental army now had 16,000 troops, and three-quarters of them came from Massachusetts. Parliament was amazed when word of the battles reached England. The prime minister, Lord North, immediately sent more troops to Boston. They arrived in Boston in May 1775, under the direction of generals William Howe, John Burgoyne, and Henry Clinton. The Massachusetts Provincial Congress was a temporary organization of colonial leaders that had been formed to act as a temporary governing body for Massachusetts. The congress met at Concord and declared the British march to be an act of war.

The colonists organized to defend Boston by occupying the high points in the hills around the city. The rebel militia established its strongest defensive position on Breed's Hill on the Charlestown peninsula. On June 17, General Howe and 2,500 British "redcoats" twice attacked this position, and twice were forced to retreat. They suffered heavy losses before finally forcing the Americans away. The misnamed Battle of Bunker Hill left 1,054 British and 441 Americans dead. This convinced the Americans they could stand up to the supposedly superior British forces, which withdrew from Boston in 1776.

The War Rages On

For nearly eight years, the war raged throughout the colonies. Although it started in Massachusetts, much of the subsequent war was fought in the other colonies. Massachusetts continued to play a significant role, however. The British received their supplies by ship, and Washington knew that capturing these ships would both hurt the British and provide supplies for the Continental army. He turned to the ships of Boston to form the basis of the Continental navy. In addition, the Continental Congress and the state of Massachusetts commissioned 1,600 Massachusetts ships as privateers. A privateer is essentially a legal pirate. The captains of these ships were granted the right to attack and capture British vessels and the cargo they carried.

Two types of soldiers from Massachusetts fought in the Revolutionary War. The first type were regular members of the Continental army gathered from volunteers to meet the quota set for the colony by the Continental Congress. In addition, the Massachusetts state militia was made up of local people in each town. Every able-bodied man was expected to participate in this militia when needed. A number of prominent men from Massachusetts also played a diplomatic role in the war, attempting

This is a hand-colored print of Boston Harbor by Paul Revere. The print depicts British naval ships of war in the foreground arriving in 1768 to put down the colonial rebellion. This print gives a sense of how Boston Harbor looked during the Revolutionary War period, when it served as a crucial battleground. Boston Harbor during the eighteenth century was made up of forty wharves, numerous shipyards, and six ropewalks.

to get aid and support for the American cause. For instance, John Adams served as a diplomat negotiating with the French and Dutch.

The End of War

In 1781, George Washington succeeded in obtaining naval support from the French with the diplomatic help of the Marquis de Lafayette and other high-ranking French noblemen. On August 30, 1781, with the assistance of the French, Washington defeated the head of British forces in America, Lord Cornwallis, at Yorktown,

Surrender of Lord Cornwallis at Yorktown, Virginia, October 19, 1781 was painted by John Trumbull, a soldier and aide to George Washington, in 1786. The first impression of this painting is that the British soldiers are on the left side holding the white flag of surrender. These are actually French soldiers, and the flag is that of the royal family of France at the time. The British soldiers are marching at the center. General George Washington and the American troops are to the right. The painting depicts the three principal officers coming together: Washington, General Rochambeau, and General Lincoln *(center)* who was sent by Lord Cornwallis.

Virginia. A few months later, Britain opened peace negotiations with the Americans.

John Adams, in his diplomatic role, played a key part in these negotiations. On November 30, 1782, the British and Americans signed a tentative peace treaty in Paris, which was finalized in April 1783. The thirteen American colonies had become the new, independent nation known as the United States of America.

CHAPTER 6

The war had a devastating effect on the Massachusetts economy. Prior to the war, Massachusetts had been a prosperous colony with a thriving mercantile import and export industry, as well as large fishing and whaling fleets. The war hit Massachusetts hard in three ways. First, trade was disrupted by the war and the British navy had blocked access to the harbor, effectively cutting off these major sources of the colony's income. Second, the war had brought with it great expenses, which in turn had resulted in heavy taxes being imposed on the citizens of the state. Third, in response to the need for cash, the Continental Congress had started to print paper money, setting its value at forty papers being equal to one gold or silver dollar (the common currency of the time). However, people lacked faith in the paper money, and the exchange rate quickly rose to 100 to 1. Eventually, the paper notes became worthless. Thus, people who had accepted them lost a great deal of money.

Forming a New Nation

Shays's Rebellion

Hardest hit by the economic impact of the war were the farmers and working class. Many farmers and laborers, especially those in the less-prosperous central and western part of the state, were overwhelmed by debts and taxes. Many of them were brought into court by those merchants and lenders to whom they owed money. All too often the court ordered the sale of their property to meet their debts and even sometimes sent the debtors to prison for not paying them.

In response, angry farmers decided to force the courts to close. The rebellion started on August 29, 1786. Two veteran officers of the

Daniel Shays (*left*) and Joe Shattuck (*right*) are pictured on the cover of the 1787 *Bickerstaff's Boston Almanack*. Shays was a veteran of the Revolutionary War and a farmer. He led indebted farmers in the tax rebellion eventually named after him, and was put down by government forces. Though the rebels were sentenced to death for treason, they were eventually pardoned. The rebellion was seen as a need for a strong central government.

Revolutionary War, Daniel Shays (1747–1825) of Pelham and Luke Day of West Springfield, then rose to lead the insurgents. The anti-court movement grew, and kept both the county court at Worcester and the state supreme court from holding sessions. Eventually, Boston property owners became so frightened of the ever-growing mobs that they provided money to the state treasury to raise a militia. On February 4, 1787, at Petersham, this militia, under the direction of General Benjamin Lincoln, faced off against the main part of Shays's band. Many of Shays's followers were arrested, tried for treason, and sentenced to death (all were eventually pardoned, however), and the rest fled. Even though the uprising failed, it forced the courts to take a more reasonable approach to dealing with debtors. For example, all debtors in prison were freed.

By 1788, business conditions began to improve. The trading, fishing, and shipbuilding industries began to recover. New textile manufacturing and iron-working industries were started. A general improvement in the economy alleviated the worst problems faced by farmers and other workers. However, the fact that a popular uprising like Shays's Rebellion could occur emphasized, in the minds of the wealthy people who filled most of the government offices, the need for a strong central government.

A Perpetual Union

Once the British had left American shores, the question arose of how to govern the people of the new country. In 1781, Maryland had become the last of the original thirteen colonies to sign the Articles of Confederation. These articles, drafted by the Second Continental Congress in 1777, and subsequently approved by the individual states, created a perpetual union of states and set up a congress in which each state had a representative with one vote. However, the central government, the congress itself, could only pass laws. It had no courts to enforce its laws. In addition, it could ask for monetary contributions from the states, but it could not demand them, nor could it mint money. There were also a large number of war debts to repay. It was vital that the country develop a stronger central government than the one outlined in the Articles of Confederation.

In 1787, the Constitutional Convention met in Philadelphia to hammer out the rules that would govern the new United States of America. The formal Constitution was also drawn up. The Constitution had to be ratified (or formally accepted) by each state. In January 1788, a convention was held in Massachusetts to consider it.

Massachusetts and the Bill of Rights

Many of the representatives to the Massachusetts convention objected to the proposed federal Constitution. Chief among the

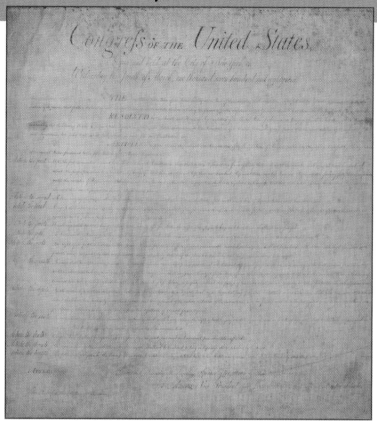

Pictured above is the Bill of Rights. The creation of these amendments led to the plan for central government to go into operation. At least nine of the thirteen new states had to approve the Constitution. As Virginia and New York were the largest at the time, however, their approvals were crucial. Delaware was the first to approve the Constitution in December 1787. North Carolina and Rhode Island disapproved until after the other states approved.

issues raised were the lack of guarantees protecting citizens' civil rights, freedom of the press, right to a fair trial, and the like. Those attending did not want to see a repeat of the type of oppression they'd experienced at the hands of the British.

John Hancock eventually suggested that the Constitution should be accepted, providing that a series of amendments protecting such individual rights was added to it. Massachusetts thus became the sixth state to accept the Constitution and the first to

John Hancock was one of the richest men in Massachusetts. He served as governor of Massachusetts from 1780 to 1785. He sat out one term, but was reelected and proved to be lenient to Daniel Shays's rebels. The economic hardships of Massachusetts, as well as the suffering of the other states, made Hancock receptive to a strong central government. Presiding over the Massachusetts convention for the ratification of the Constitution, he first pointed out the respectable character of the authors of the draft. After several weeks of debate, he resumed his place as president and made a rousing speech recommending the amendments.

accept it on the condition that amendments be attached to it. Thus, Massachusetts, the state founded by those who had left their homes in search of the freedom to practice their religion and whose radicals had been pioneers in the fight for individual rights, came full circle to play a key role in the development of the Bill of Rights. These first ten amendments to the Constitution protect and guarantee our most basic freedoms today. These freedoms include the right to free speech, religious freedom, and protection against secret searches and arrest.

TIMELINE

1498 —— John Cabot sails up the coast of New England.

1602 —— The explorer Bartholomew Gosnold gives Cape Cod its name.

1609 —— Massachusetts Bay is explored by Henry Hudson.

1614 —— Massachusetts Bay is explored by John Smith.

1620 —— The *Mayflower* arrives, and the Pilgrims establish New Plymouth.

1629 —— The Puritans form the Massachusetts Bay Colony.
–1630

1636 —— The Pequot War occurs.
–1637

1675 —— King Philip's War occurs.
–1676

1756 —— The French and Indian War takes place.
–1763

1764 —— The Sugar Act is passed by Parliament.

1765 —— The Stamp Act is passed by Parliament. The Sons of Liberty is formed.

1767—— The Townshend Acts are passed by Parliament.

1770 —— The Boston Massacre occurs.

1772 —— Boston Committee of Correspondence is formed.

1773 —— The Tea Act is enacted by Parliament. The Boston Tea Party takes place.

1774 —— The Coercive Acts are passed by Parliament. The British occupy Boston. The Suffolk Resolves are drafted.

1775 —— The battles of Lexington and Concord occur.

1776 —— The British evacuate Boston.

1780 —— The Constitution of the Commonwealth of Massachusetts is ratified. John Hancock is elected as the first governor of the state.

1783 —— The Treaty of Paris ends the Revolutionary War.

1786 –1787 —— Shays's Rebellion lasts for six months, beginning on August 29, 1786.

1788 —— Massachusetts ratifies the federal Constitution and becomes the sixth state to join the Union. Massachusetts representatives suggest the amendments that become the Bill of Rights.

PRIMARY SOURCE TRANSCRIPTIONS

Page 19: Introduction to *Of Plymouth Plantation: The Journal of William Bradford*

Transcription

And first of the occasion and inducements thereunto; the which, that I may truly unfold, I must begin at the very root and rise of the same. The which I shall endeavor to manifest in a plain style, with singular regard unto the simple truth in all things; at least as near as my slender judgment can attain the same.

Excerpt from William Bradford's *Of Plymouth Plantation* **describing the disbursement of the population of the colony and of New England to form new towns and congregations during the early 1630s:**

Transcription (Contemporary English Translation)

Also the people of the plantation began to grow in their outward estates, by reason of the flowing of many people into the country, especially into the Bay of the Massachusetts; by which means corn and cattle rose to a great price, by which many were much enriched, and commodities grew plentiful; and yet in other regards this benefit turned to their hurt, and this accession of strength to their weakness. For now as their stocks increased, and the increase was vendible, there was no longer any holding them together, but now they must of necessity go to their great lots; they could not otherwise keep their cattle; and having oxen grown, they must have land for plowing and tillage. And no man now thought he could live, except he had cattle and a great deal of ground to keep them; all striving to increase their stocks. By which means they were scattered all over the bay, quickly, and the town, in which they lived compactly till now, was left very thin, and in a short time almost desolate. And if this had been it, it had been less, though to much; but the church must also be divided, and those who had lived to long together in Christian and comfortable fellowship must now part and suffer many divisions. First, those that lived on their lots on the other side of the bay (called Duxberie) they could no longer bring their wives and children to the public worship and church meetings here . . .

Page 22: Petition for bail from accused witches, ca 1692:

Transcription (Contemporary English Translation)

To the Honourable Governor and Council and General Assembly now sitting at Boston

The humble petition of us whose names are subscribed hereunto now prisoners at Ipswich humbly [show], that some of us have been in the prison many months, and some of us many weeks, who are charged with witchcraft, and not being conscious to ourselves of any guilt of that nature lying upon our consciences; our earnest request is that seeing the winter is so far come on that it can not be expected that we should be tried during this winter season, that we may be released out of prison for the present upon bail to answer what we are charged with in the spring. For we are not in this unwilling nor afraid to abide the trial before any Judicature appointed in convenient season of any crime of that nature; we hope you will put on the bowels of compassion so far as to consider of our suffering condition in the present state we are in, being likely to perish with cold in lying longer in prison in this cold season of the year, some of us being aged either about or near fourscore some though younger yet being with child, and one nursing a child not ten weeks old yet, and all of us weak and infirmed at the best, and one fettered with irons for a half year and all most destroyed with so long an imprisonment. Thus hoping you will grant us a release at the present that we be not left to perish in this miserable condition we shall always pray [omitted word].

> Widow Penny. Widow Vincent. Widow Prince.
> Goodwife Greene of Havarell, the wife of Hugh
> Roe of Cape Anne, Mehitabel Downing. The Wife
> of Timothy Day, Goodwife Dicer of Piscatagua
> Hanah Brumidge of Havarell Rachel Hafield
> besides three or four men

Page 32: Obituary of four of the five slain men of the Boston Massacre from the *Boston Gazette and Country Journal*, March 12, 1770.

Transcription (Contemporary English Translation)

Last Thursday, agreeable to a general Request of the Inhabitants, and by the Consent of Parents and Friends, were carried to their Grave in Succession, the Bodies of Samuel Gray, Samuel Maverick, James Caldwell, and Crispus Attucks, the unhappy Victims who fell in the bloody Massacre of the Monday Evening preceding!

On this occasion most of the shops in town were shut, all the bells ordered to toll a solemn peal, as were also those in the neighboring towns of Charleston, Roxbury, etc. The procession began to move between the hours of 4 and 5 in the afternoon; two of the unfortunate sufferers, Mess. James Caldwell and Crispus Attucks, who were strangers, born from Faneuil-Hall, attended by a numerous train of persons of all ranks; and the other two. Mr. Samuel Gray, from the house of M. Benjamin Gray, (his brother) on the northside of the Exchange, and Mr. Maverick, from the house of his distressed mother Mrs. Mary Maverick, in Union-Street, each followed by their respective relations and friends: The several hearses forming a junction in King-Street, the theatre of the inhuman tragedy proceeded from there through the Main-Street, lengthened by an immense concourse of people, so numerous as to be obliged to follow in ranks of six, and brought up by a long train of carriages belonging to the principal gentry of the town. The bodies were deposited in one vault in the middle burying-ground: The aggravated circumstances of their death, the distress and sorrow visible in every countenance, together with the peculiar solemnity with which the whole funeral was conducted surpass description.

GLOSSARY

Bill of Rights The first ten amendments to the U.S. Constitution guaranteeing citizens' basic rights.

circular A pamphlet intended for wide distribution.

Committees of Correspondence Legislative committees charged with supplying news to the legislatures of other colonies.

land grant A legal document giving people the right to settle on a particular piece of land.

nonimportation agreement An agreement not to import goods from a particular country, such as England.

Pilgrims A group of religious dissenters in sixteenth- and seventeenth-century England who wanted to replace the Church of England with a new, purer church. Also called Separatists.

privateer The captain of a sailing vessel given official authority by a government to attack and capture the ships of an enemy nation.

Puritans A religious sect in sixteenth- and seventeenth-century England that wanted to purify the Church of England of its Catholic practices.

Reformation The replacing of the Catholic Church in England with the Protestant Church of England by King Henry VIII.

sacrament An action that brings God's favor to the doer, such as baptism.

FOR MORE INFORMATION

Web Sites

Due to the changing nature of Internet links, The Rosen Publishing Group, Inc., has developed an online list of Web sites related to the subject of this book. This site is updated regularly. Please use this link to access the list:

http://www.rosenlinks.com/pstc/mass

FOR FURTHER READING

Bradford, William. *Of Plymouth Plantation 1620-1647*. New York, NY: Alfred A. Knopf, Inc. 2002.

Daugherty, James. *The Landing of the Pilgrims*. New York, NY: Random House, 1987.

Dow, George Francis. *Every Day Life in the Massachusetts Bay Colony*. New York, NY: Dover, 1988.

Grace, Catherine O'Neill, Peter Arenstam, and John Kemp. *Mayflower 1620: A New Look at a Pilgrim Voyage*. New York, NY: National Geographic, 2003.

Gross, Robert A. *The Minutemen and Their World*. New York, NY: Hill and Wang, 2001.

Haskins, Jim, Cox Clinton, and Brenda Wilkinson. *Black Stars of Colonial Times and the Revolutionary War: African Americans Who Lived Their Dreams*. New York, NY: Wiley, 2002.

January, Brendan. *Revolutionary War*. Minneapolis, MN: Rebound by Sagebrush, 2002.

Jones, Veda. *Samuel Adams: Patriot*. Minneapolis, MN: Rebound by Sagebrush, 2002.

Knight, James E. *Salem Days: Life in a Colonial Seaport*. Mahwah, NJ: Troll Associates, 1982.

Rappaport, Doreen, Greg Call, and Joan Verniero. *Victory or Death!: Stories of the American Revolution*. New York, NY: HarperCollins, 2003.

Scheer, George F., and Hugh F. Rankin. *Rebels & Redcoats: The American Revolution Through the Eyes of Those Who Fought and Lived It*. New York, NY: Da Capo Press, 1987.

Thompson, Kathleen. *Massachusetts*. New York, NY: Raintree Steck-Vaughn, 1996.

BIBLIOGRAPHY

America's Homepage, "Wampanoag Tribes." Retrieved September 1, 2004 (http://pilgrims.net/native_americans).

Bradford, William. *Of Plymouth Plantation*. New York, NY: McGraw-Hill, 1981.

Commonwealth Museum, "Massachusetts History Timeline." Retrieved September 1, 2004 (http://www.sec.state.man.us/mus/musexe/mustim/timeidx.htm).

Dow, George Francis. *Every Day Life in the Massachusetts Bay Colony*. New York, NY: Dover, 1988.

Gross, Robert A. *The Minutemen and Their World*. New York, NY: Hill & Wang, 2001.

Hart, Albert Bushnell, ed. *England in America 1580-1652*, Vol. 4 (The American Nation, A History: From Original Sources by Associated Scholars). New York, NY: Harper, 1904.

Hart, Albert Bushnell, ed. *Provincial America 1690-1740*, Vol. 6 (The American Nation, A History: From Original Sources by Associated Scholars). New York, NY: Harper, 1905.

Hart, Albert Bushnell, ed. *The Confederation and the Constitution 1783-1789*, Vol. 10 (The American Nation, A History: From Original Sources by Associated Scholars). New York, NY: Harper, 1905.

Logan, Samuel T., Jr., "The Pilgrims and Puritans: Total Reformation for the Glory of God." Retrieved September 1, 2004 (http://www.puritansermons.com/banner/logan1.htm).

Maier, Pauline. *The Old Revolutionaries: Political Lives in the Age of Samuel Adams*. New York, NY: Vintage, 1980.

Reid, William J,. and Herbert G. Regan. *Massachusetts: History and Government of the Bay State*. New York, NY: Oxford Book Company, 1956.

Scheer, George F., and Hugh F. Rankin. *Rebels & Redcoats: The American Revolution Through the Eyes of Those Who Fought and Lived It*. New York, NY: Da Capo, 1987.

Schlesinger, Arthur M., and Dixon Ryan Fox, eds. *A History of American Life*, Vol. 2. (The First Americans) New York, NY: Macmillan, 1927.

Teacheroz.com. "Discovery, Exploration, Colonies, & Revolution." Retrieved September 1, 2004 (www.teacheroz.com/colonies.htm).

Yale Law School. "The Avalon Project." Retrieved September 1, 2004 (http://www.yale.edu/lawweb/avalon).

PRIMARY SOURCE IMAGE LIST

Title Page: *A Westerly View of the Colledges in Cambridge New England*, 1767. An engraving by Paul Revere housed at the American Antiquarian Society.

Page 9: The title page of *New Britannia, Offering Most Excellent Fruites by Planting in Virginia*. Printed in London in 1609 by Samuel Macham, part of the Library of Congress's American Memory Collection.

Page 11: Map of the northeast coast of North America, 1607, by Samuel de Champlain (1567-1635). This facsimile is housed in the Library of Congress.

Page 12: The passenger list of the *Mayflower* can be found in William Bradford's *Of Plymouth Plantation* at the State Library of Massachusetts. Inset portrait of Edward Winslow painted in London in 1651 by an anonymous artist. Housed in the Pilgrim Hall Museum.

Page 19: *Of Plymouth Plantation*, the journal of William Bradford, is housed at the State Library in the State House, Boston, MA.

Page 20: *Ornatus Muliebris Anglicanus* was printed by Overton in London in 1648. It is located in the British Library, Early Printed Collections, London, England.

Page 22: Petition for bail from accused witches, circa 1692, is housed in the John Davis Batchelder Autograph Collection, Library of Congress Manuscript Division.

Page 25: Portrait of Edmund Burke by James Northcote (1746-1831) housed at Royal Albert Memorial Museum, Exeter, Devon, United Kingdom. Portrait of Frederick North, second Earl of Guildford, by Nathaniel Dance in 1755, the National Portrait Gallery, London, England.

Page 26: Engraving of *The Town of Boston in New England* by John Bonner, 1722. Norman B. Levenhal Map Collection, Boston, MA.

Page 28: Title page of the first edition of the Stamp Act and embossed stamp that was created at time of the Stamp Act, 1765. Part of the Library of Congress collection.

Page 29: Portrait of Samuel Adams circa 1770-1772, located at the New York Historical Society, New York, NY.

Page 30: Broadside calling for boycott by Sons of Liberty, January 1770, part of the Library of Congress's American Memory Collection.

Page 32: Obituaries of four slain in the Boston Massacre from *The Boston Gazette and Country Journal*, March 12, 1770. Engraved by Paul Revere, housed in the Library of Congress.

Page 34: Tea leaves collected by T. M. Harris at Dorchester Neck, December 1773. Artifact is housed at the Massachusetts Historical Society, Boston, MA.

Page 37: Carpenter's Hall in Philadelphia, PA, by anonymous artist. Housed at the New York Public Library.

Page 39: Portrait of Paul Revere, 1768, oil on canvas by John Singleton Copley. Housed at the Museum of Fine Arts, Boston, MA.

Page 41: Plate II (of four). *A View of the Town of Concord*, copper engraving by Amos Doolittle, 1775. The New York Public Library.

Page 46: *Surrender of Lord Cornwallis at Yorktown, Virginia, October 19, 1781* by John Trumbull in 1786 to 1787, United States Capitol Historical Society.

Page 48: *Bickerstaff's Boston Almanack of 1787* (c. 1787), National Picture Gallery, Smithsonian Institution.

Page 50: The Bill of Rights, created March 4, 1789, is on permanent display in the Rotunda of the National Archives Building, Washington, D.C.

Page 51: John Hancock (1737-1793), circa 1816, oil on canvas by Samuel Finley Breese Morse after John Singleton Copley. This portrait is in the collection of Independence National Historic Park, Philadelphia, PA.

INDEX

About the Author

Jeri Freedman has a BA from Harvard University. She is the author of a number of other non-fiction books published by Rosen Publishing, as well as several plays and, under the name Foxxe, is the coauthor of two alternate history science-fiction novels. She lives in Boston.

Photo Credits

Cover, pp. 12 (right), 17 (top) Courtesy of Pilgrim Hall Museum, Plymouth, Massachusetts; pp. 1, 45 Courtesy, American Antiquarian Society; pp. 5, 46 Architect of the Capitol; pp. 7, 30, 32 (right) © Getty Images; p. 9 © Bettmann/Corbis; p. 11 Library of Congress Geography and Map Division; pp. 12 (left), 19 Courtesy of the State Library of Massachusetts; pp. 15, 32 (left) Library of Congress Prints and Photographs Division; p. 17 (bottom) Courtesy of Haffenreffer Museum of Anthropology, Brown University; p. 20 Art & Architecture Collection, Miriam and Ira D. Wallach Division of Art, Prints and Photographs, The New York Public Library, Astor, Lenox and Tilden Foundations; p. 22 (left) Library of Congress Manuscript Division; p. 22 (right) Examination of a Witch by T.H. Matteson, Oil painting 1853. Photograph Courtesy of Peabody Essex Museum; p. 25 (left) Royal Albert Memorial Museum, Exeter, Devon, UK/Bridgeman Art Library; p. 25 (right) National Portrait Gallery, London; p. 26 I.N. Phelps Stokes Collection, Miriam and Ira D. Wallach Division of Art, Prints and Photographs, The New York Public Library, Astor, Lenox and Tilden Foundations; p. 28 Picture History; pp. 29, 39 Photograph © 2005 Museum of Fine Art, Boston; p. 34 (top) Private Collection/Bridgeman Art Library; p. 34 (bottom) © Massachusetts Historical Society, Boston, MA, USA/Bridgeman Art Library; p. 37 The New York Public Library/Art Resource, NY; p. 41 Print Collection, Miriam and Ira D. Wallach Division of Art, Prints and Photographs, The New York Public Library, Astor, Lenox and Tilden Foundations; p. 42 courtesy of Jeri Freedman; p. 48 National Portrait Gallery, Smithsonian Institution/Art Resource, NY; p. 50 National Archives and Records Administration; p. 51 Independence National Historical Park.

Editor: Leigh Ann Cobb; **Photo Researcher**: Sheri Liberman